W9-AUN-645

SELECTED
POEMS
OF
Emily
Dickinson

FALL RIVER PRESS

New York

FALL RIVER PRESS

New York

An Imprint of Sterling Publishing Co., Inc.
1166 Avenue of the Americas
New York, NY 10036

This 2016 edition printed for Barnes & Noble
by Sterling Publishing Co., Inc.

ISBN 978-1-4351-6256-3

Barnes & Noble, Inc.
122 Fifth Avenue
New York, NY 10011

Manufactured in China

6 8 10 9 7 5

www.sterlingpublishing.com

Cover design by David Ter-Avanasyen

CONTENTS

NOTE ON THE TEXT

The texts for the poems in this volume are taken primarily from the following editions:

Dickinson, Emily. *The Single Hound: Poems of a Lifetime.* Boston: Little, Brown, and Company, 1915.

Todd, Mabel Loomis (ed.) *Poems by Emily Dickinson: Third Series.* Boston: Little, Brown, and Company, 1896.

Todd, Mabel Loomis and Higginson, T. W. (eds.) *Poems by Emily Dickinson.* Boston: Roberts Brothers, 1891.

Todd, Mabel Loomis and Higginson, T. W. (eds.) *Poems by Emily Dickinson: Second Series.* Boston: Roberts Brothers, 1892.

THIS IS my letter to the world,
That never wrote to me,—
The simple news that Nature told,
With tender majesty.

Her message is committed
To hands I cannot see;
For love of her, sweet countrymen,
Judge tenderly of me!

————⟨⟩————

I'M NOBODY! Who are you?
Are you nobody, too?
Then there's a pair of us—don't tell!
They'd banish us, you know.

How dreary to be somebody!
How public, like a frog
To tell your name the livelong day
To an admiring bog!

————⟨⟩————

SUCCESS IS counted sweetest
By those who ne'er succeed.
To comprehend a nectar
Requires sorest need.

Not one of all the purple host
Who took the flag to-day
Can tell the definition,
So clear, of victory,

As he, defeated, dying,
On whose forbidden ear
The distant strains of triumph
Break, agonized and clear.

A WOUNDED DEER leaps highest,
I've heard the hunter tell;
'Tis but the ecstasy of death,
And then the brake is still.

The smitten rock that gushes,
The trampled steel that springs:
A cheek is always redder
Just where the hectic stings!

Mirth is the mail of anguish,
In which it caution arm,
Lest anybody spy the blood
And "You're hurt" exclaim!

THE HEART asks pleasure first,
And then, excuse from pain;
And then, those little anodynes
That deaden suffering;

And then, to go to sleep;
And then, if it should be
The will of its Inquisitor,
The liberty to die.

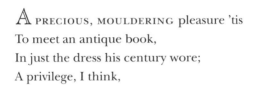

A PRECIOUS, MOULDERING pleasure 'tis
To meet an antique book,
In just the dress his century wore;
A privilege, I think,

His venerable hand to take,
And warming in our own,
A passage back, or two, to make
To times when he was young.

His quaint opinions to inspect,
His knowledge to unfold
On what concerns our mutual mind,
The literature of old;

What interested scholars most,
What competitions ran
When Plato was a certainty,
And Sophocles a man;

When Sappho was a living girl,
And Beatrice wore
The gown that Dante deified.
Facts, centuries before,

He traverses familiar,
As one should come to town
And tell you all your dreams were true:
He lived where dreams were born.

His presence is enchantment,
You beg him not to go;
Old volumes shake their vellum heads
And tantalize, just so.

———— ⟿ ————

MUCH MADNESS is divinest sense
To a discerning eye;
Much sense the starkest madness.
'Tis the majority
In this, as all, prevails.
Assent, and you are sane;
Demur,—you're straightway dangerous,
And handled with a chain.

———— ⟿ ————

I ASKED NO other thing,
No other was denied.
I offered Being for it;
The mighty merchant smiled.

Brazil? He twirled a button.
Without a glance my way:
"But, madam, is there nothing else
That we can show to-day?"

THE SOUL selects her own society,
Then shuts the door;
On her divine majority
Obtrude no more.

Unmoved, she notes the chariot's pausing
At her low gate;
Unmoved, an emperor is kneeling
Upon her mat.

I've known her from an ample nation
Choose one;
Then close the valves of her attention
Like stone.

I KNOW SOME lonely houses off the road
A robber'd like the look of,—
Wooden barred,
And windows hanging low,
Inviting to
A portico,

Where two could creep:
One hand the tools,
The other peep
To make sure all's asleep.
Old-fashioned eyes,
Not easy to surprise!

How orderly the kitchen'd look by night,
With just a clock,—
But they could gag the tick,
And mice won't bark;
And so the walls don't tell,
None will.

A pair of spectacles ajar just stir—
An almanac's aware.
Was it the mat winked,
Or a nervous star?
The moon slides down the stair
To see who's there.

There's plunder,—where?
Tankard, or spoon,
Earring, or stone,
A watch, some ancient brooch
To match the grandmamma,
Staid sleeping there.

Day rattles, too,
Stealth's slow;
The sun has got as far
As the third sycamore.
Screams chanticleer,
"Who's there?"

And echoes, trains away,
Sneer—"Where?"
While the old couple, just astir,
Think that the sunrise left the door ajar!

To fight aloud is very brave,
But gallanter, I know,
Who charge within the bosom,
The cavalry of woe.

Who win, and nations do not see,
Who fall, and none observe,
Whose dying eyes no country
Regards with patriot love.

We trust, in plumed procession,
For such the angels go,
Rank after rank, with even feet
And uniforms of snow.

———————

PAIN HAS an element of blank;
It cannot recollect
When it began, or if there were
A day when it was not.

It has no future but itself,
Its infinite realms contain
Its past, enlightened to perceive
New periods of pain.

———————

I TASTE A liquor never brewed,
From tankards scooped in pearl;
Not all the vats upon the Rhine
Yield such an alcohol!

Inebriate of air am I,
And debauchee of dew,
Reeling, through endless summer days,
From inns of molten blue.

When landlords turn the drunken bee
Out of the foxglove's door,
When butterflies renounce their drams,
I shall but drink the more!

Till seraphs swing their snowy hats,
And saints to windows run,
To see the little tippler
Leaning against the sun!

———◦◦◦———

HE ATE and drank the precious words,
His spirit grew robust;
He knew no more that he was poor,
Nor that his frame was dust.
He danced along the dingy days,
And this bequest of wings
Was but a book. What liberty
A loosened spirit brings!

———◦◦◦———

THE NEAREST dream recedes, unrealized.
The heaven we chase
Like the June bee
Before the school-boy
Invites the race,
Stoops to an easy clover—
Dips—evades—teases—deploys;

Then to the royal clouds
Lifts his light pinnace
Heedless of the boy
Staring, bewildered, at the mocking sky.

Homesick for steadfast honey,
Ah! the bee flies not
That brews that rare variety.

———⟨∞⟩———

I FOUND THE phrase to every thought
I ever had, but one;
And that defies me,—as a hand
Did try to chalk the sun

To races nurtured in the dark;—
How would your own begin?
Can blaze be done in cochineal,
Or noon in mazarin?

———⟨∞⟩———

HOPE IS the thing with feathers
That perches in the soul,
And sings the tune without the words,
And never stops at all,

And sweetest in the gale is heard;
And sore must be the storm
That could abash the little bird
That kept so many warm.

I've heard it in the chillest land,
And on the strangest sea;
Yet, never, in extremity,
It asked a crumb of me.

———◦◦———

DARE YOU see a soul at the white heat?
Then crouch within the door.
Red is the fire's common tint;
But when the vivid ore

Has sated flame's conditions,
Its quivering substance plays
Without a color but the light
Of unanointed blaze.

Least village boasts its blacksmith,
Whose anvil's even din
Stands symbol for the finer forge
That soundless tugs within,

Refining these impatient ores
With hammer and with blaze,
Until the designated light
Repudiate the forge.

———◦◦———

I CAN WADE grief,
Whole pools of it,—
I'm used to that.
But the least push of joy
Breaks up my feet,
And I tip—drunken.
Let no pebble smile,
'Twas the new liquor,—
That was all!

Power is only pain,
Stranded, through discipline,
Till weights will hang.
Give balm to giants,
And they'll wilt, like men.
Give Himmaleh,—
They'll carry him!

THE THOUGHT beneath so slight a film
Is more distinctly seen,—
As laces just reveal the surge,
Or mists the Apennine.

I LIKE TO see it lap the miles,
And lick the valleys up,
And stop to feed itself at tanks;
And then, prodigious, step

Around a pile of mountains,
And, supercilious, peer
In shanties by the sides of roads;
And then a quarry pare

To fit its sides, and crawl between,
Complaining all the while
In horrid, hooting stanza;
Then chase itself down hill

And neigh like Boanerges;
Then, punctual as a star,
Stop—docile and omnipotent—
At its own stable door.

I SHOULD HAVE been too glad, I see,
Too lifted for the scant degree
Of life's penurious round;
My little circuit would have shamed
This new circumference, have blamed
The homelier time behind.

I should have been too saved, I see,
Too rescued; fear too dim to me
That I could spell the prayer
I knew so perfect yesterday,—
That scalding one, "Sabachthani",
Recited fluent here.

Earth would have been too much, I see,
And heaven not enough for me;
I should have had the joy
Without the fear to justify,—
The palm without the Calvary;
So, Saviour, crucify.

Defeat whets victory, they say;
The reefs in old Gethsemane
Endear the shore beyond.
'Tis beggars banquets best define;
'Tis thirsting vitalizes wine,—
Faith faints to understand.

VICTORY COMES late,
And is held low to freezing lips
Too rapt with frost
To take it.

How sweet it would have tasted,
Just a drop!
Was God so economical?
His table's spread too high for us
Unless we dine on tip-toe.
Crumbs fit such little mouths,
Cherries suit robins;
The eagle's golden breakfast
Strangles them.
God keeps his oath to sparrows,
Who of little love
Know how to starve!

———⟊———

Faith is a fine invention
For gentlemen who see;
But microscopes are prudent
In an emergency!

———⟊———

Each life converges to some centre
Expressed or still;
Exists in every human nature
A goal,

Admitted scarcely to itself, it may be,
Too fair
For credibility's temerity
To dare.

Adored with caution, as a brittle heaven,
To reach
Were hopeless as the rainbow's raiment
To touch,

Yet persevered toward, surer for the distance;
How high
Unto the saints' slow diligence
The sky!

Ungained, it may be, by life's low venture,
But then,
Eternity enables the endeavoring
Again.

BEFORE I got my eye put out,
I liked as well to see
As other creatures that have eyes,
And know no other way.

But were it told to me, to-day,
That I might have the sky
For mine, I tell you that my heart
Would split, for size of me.

The meadows mine, the mountains mine,—
All forests, stintless stars,
As much of noon as I could take
Between my finite eyes.

The motions of the dipping birds,
The lightning's jointed road,
For mine to look at when I liked,—
The news would strike me dead!

So, safer, guess, with just my soul
Upon the window-pane
Where other creatures put their eyes,
Incautious of the sun.

WHEN I hoped I feared,
Since I hoped I dared;
Everywhere alone
As a church remain;
Spectre cannot harm,
Serpent cannot charm;
He deposes doom,
Who hath suffered him.

PRAYER IS the little implement
Through which men reach
Where presence is denied them.
They fling their speech

By means of it in God's ear;
If then He hear,
This sums the apparatus
Comprised in prayer.

I KNOW THAT he exists
Somewhere, in silence.
He has hid his rare life
From our gross eyes.

'Tis in instant's play,
'Tis a fond ambush,
Just to make bliss
Earn her own surprise!

But should the play
Prove piercing earnest,
Should the glee glaze
In death's stiff stare,

Would not the fun
Look too expensive?
Would not the jest
Have crawled too far?

MUSICIANS WRESTLE everywhere:
All day, among the crowded air,
I hear the silver strife;
And—waking long before the dawn—
Such transport breaks upon the town
I think it that "new life!"

It is not bird, it has no nest;
Nor band, in brass and scarlet dressed,
Nor tambourine, nor man;
It is not hymn from pulpit read,—
The morning stars the treble led
On time's first afternoon!

Some say it is the spheres at play!
Some say that bright majority
Of vanished dames and men!
Some think it service in the place
Where we, with late, celestial face,
Please God, shall ascertain!

———⟩⟨———

My life closed twice before its close;
It yet remains to see
If Immortality unveil
A third event to me,

So huge, so hopeless to conceive,
As these that twice befell.
Parting is all we know of heaven,
And all we need of hell.

———⟩⟨———

THERE IS no frigate like a book
To take us lands away,
Nor any coursers like a page
Of prancing poetry.

This traverse may the poorest take
Without oppress of toll;
How frugal is the chariot
That bears a human soul!

———❧———

I FELT A cleavage in my mind
As if my brain had split;
I tried to match it, seam by seam,
But could not make them fit.

The thought behind I strove to join
Unto the thought before,
But sequence ravelled out of reach
Like balls upon a floor.

———❧———

OUR LIVES are Swiss,—
So still, so cool,
Till, some odd afternoon,
The Alps neglect their curtains,
And we look farther on.

Italy stands the other side,
While, like a guard between,
The solemn Alps,
The siren Alps,
Forever intervene!

———◦୨୧◦———

THE BRAIN is wider than the sky,
For, put them side by side,
The one the other will include
With ease, and you beside.

The brain is deeper than the sea,
For, hold them, blue to blue,
The one the other will absorb,
As sponges, buckets do.

The brain is just the weight of God,
For, lift them, pound for pound,
And they will differ, if they do,
As syllable from sound.

———◦୨୧◦———

THE PAST is such a curious creature,
To look her in the face
A transport may reward us,
Or a disgrace.

Unarmed if any meet her,
I charge him, fly!
Her rusty ammunition
Might yet reply!

———⟋⟍———

WHAT SOFT, cherubic creatures
These gentlewomen are!
One would as soon assault a plush
Or violate a star.

Such dimity convictions,
A horror so refined
Of freckled human nature,
Of Deity ashamed,—

It's such a common glory,
A fisherman's degree!
Redemption, brittle lady,
Be so ashamed of thee.

———⟋⟍———

I STEPPED FROM plank to plank
So slow and cautiously;
The stars about my head I felt,
About my feet the sea.

I knew not but the next
Would be my final inch,—
This gave me that precarious gait
Some call experience.

At half-past three a single bird
Unto a silent sky
Propounded but a single term
Of cautious melody.

At half-past four, experiment
Had subjugated test,
And lo! her silver principle
Supplanted all the rest.

At half-past seven, element
Nor implement was seen,
And place was where the presence was,
Circumference between.

***

One of the ones that Midas touched,
Who failed to touch us all,
Was that confiding prodigal,
The blissful oriole.

So drunk, he disavows it
With badinage divine;
So dazzling, we mistake him
For an alighting mine.

A pleader, a dissembler,
An epicure, a thief,—
Betimes an oratorio,
An ecstasy in chief;

The Jesuit of orchards,
He cheats as he enchants
Of an entire attar
For his decamping wants.

The splendor of a Burmah,
The meteor of birds,
Departing like a pageant
Of ballads and of bards.

I never thought that Jason sought
For any golden fleece;
But then I am a rural man,
With thoughts that make for peace.

But if there were a Jason,
Tradition suffer me
Behold his lost emolument
Upon the apple-tree.

I DREADED THAT first robin so,
But he is mastered now,
And I'm accustomed to him grown,—
He hurts a little, though.

I thought if I could only live
Till that first shout got by,
Not all pianos in the woods
Had power to mangle me.

I dared not meet the daffodils,
For fear their yellow gown
Would pierce me with a fashion
So foreign to my own.

I wished the grass would hurry,
So when 'twas time to see,
He'd be too tall, the tallest one
Could stretch to look at me.

I could not bear the bees should come,
I wished they'd stay away
In those dim countries where they go:
What word had they for me?

They're here, though; not a creature failed,
No blossom stayed away
In gentle deference to me,
The Queen of Calvary.

Each one salutes me as he goes,
And I my childish plumes
Lift, in bereaved acknowledgment
Of their unthinking drums.

A ROUTE OF evanescence
With a revolving wheel;
A resonance of emerald,
A rush of cochineal;
And every blossom on the bush
Adjusts its tumbled head,—
The mail from Tunis, probably,
An easy morning's ride.

I STARTED EARLY, took my dog,
And visited the sea;
The mermaids in the basement
Came out to look at me,

And frigates in the upper floor
Extended hempen hands.
Presuming me to be a mouse
Aground, upon the sands.

But no man moved me till the tide
Went past my simple shoe,
And past my apron and my belt,
And past my bodice too,

And made as he would eat me up
As wholly as a dew
Upon a dandelion's sleeve—
And then I started too.

And he—he followed close behind;
I felt his silver heel
Upon my ankle,—then my shoes
Would overflow with pearl.

Until we met the solid town,
No man he seemed to know;
And bowing with a mighty look
At me, the sea withdrew.

A BIRD CAME down the walk:
He did not know I saw;
He bit an angle-worm in halves
And ate the fellow, raw.

And then he drank a dew
From a convenient grass,
And then hopped sidewise to the wall
To let a beetle pass.

He glanced with rapid eyes
That hurried all abroad,—
They looked like frightened beads, I thought
He stirred his velvet head

Like one in danger; cautious,
I offered him a crumb,
And he unrolled his feathers
And rowed him softer home

Than oars divide the ocean,
Too silver for a seam,
Or butterflies, off banks of noon,
Leap, plashless, as they swim.

———— ⚬ ————

A NARROW FELLOW in the grass
Occasionally rides;
You may have met him,—did you not?
His notice sudden is.

The grass divides as with a comb,
A spotted shaft is seen;
And then it closes at your feet
And opens further on.

He likes a boggy acre,
A floor too cool for corn.
Yet when a child, and barefoot,
I more than once, at morn,

Have passed, I thought, a whip-lash
Unbraiding in the sun,—
When, stooping to secure it,
It wrinkled, and was gone.

Several of nature's people
I know, and they know me;
I feel for them a transport
Of cordiality;

But never met this fellow,
Attended or alone,
Without a tighter breathing,
And zero at the bone.

———※———

THERE CAME a wind like a bugle;
It quivered through the grass,
And a green chill upon the heat
So ominous did pass
We barred the windows and the doors
As from an emerald ghost;
The doom's electric moccasin
That very instant passed.

On a strange mob of panting trees,
And fences fled away,
And rivers where the houses ran
The living looked that day.
The bell within the steeple wild
The flying tidings whirled.
How much can come
And much can go,
And yet abide the world!

———※———

THE WIND tapped like a tired man,
And like a host, "Come in,"
I boldly answered; entered then
My residence within

A rapid, footless guest,
To offer whom a chair
Were as impossible as hand
A sofa to the air.

No bone had he to bind him,
His speech was like the push
Of numerous humming-birds at once
From a superior bush.

His countenance a billow,
His fingers, if he pass,
Let go a music, as of tunes
Blown tremulous in glass.

He visited, still flitting;
Then, like a timid man,
Again he tapped—'twas flurriedly—
And I became alone.

HOW HAPPY is the little stone
That rambles in the road alone,
And doesn't care about careers,
And exigencies never fears;
Whose coat of elemental brown

A passing universe put on;
And independent as the sun,
Associates or glows alone,
Fulfilling absolute decree
In casual simplicity.

———⟡———

THE WIND begun to rock the grass
With threatening tunes and low,—
He flung a menace at the earth,
A menace at the sky.

The leaves unhooked themselves from trees
And started all abroad;
The dust did scoop itself like hands
And throw away the road.

The wagons quickened on the streets,
The thunder hurried slow;
The lightning showed a yellow beak,
And then a livid claw.

The birds put up the bars to nests,
The cattle fled to barns;
There came one drop of giant rain,
And then, as if the hands

That held the dams had parted hold,
The waters wrecked the sky,
But overlooked my father's house,
Just quartering a tree.

Bring me the sunset in a cup,
Reckon the morning's flagons up,
And say how many dew;
Tell me how far the morning leaps,
Tell me what time the weaver sleeps
Who spun the breadths of blue!

Write me how many notes there be
In the new robin's ecstasy
Among astonished boughs;
How many trips the tortoise makes,
How many cups the bee partakes,—
The debauchee of dews!

Also, who laid the rainbow's piers,
Also, who leads the docile spheres
By withes of supple blue?
Whose fingers string the stalactite,
Who counts the wampum of the night,
To see that none is due?

Who built this little Alban house
And shut the windows down so close
My spirit cannot see?
Who'll let me out some gala day,
With implements to fly away,
Passing pomposity?

Farther in summer than the birds,
Pathetic from the grass,
A minor nation celebrates
Its unobtrusive mass.

No ordinance is seen,
So gradual the grace,
A pensive custom it becomes,
Enlarging loneliness.

Antiquest felt at noon
When August, burning low,
Calls forth this spectral canticle,
Repose to typify.

Remit as yet no grace,
No furrow on the glow,
Yet a druidic difference
Enhances nature now.

———

As imperceptibly as grief
The summer lapsed away,—
Too imperceptible, at last,
To seem like perfidy.

A quietness distilled,
As twilight long begun,
Or Nature, spending with herself
Sequestered afternoon.

The dusk drew earlier in,
The morning foreign shone,—
A courteous, yet harrowing grace,
As guest who would be gone.

And thus, without a wing,
Or service of a keel,
Our summer made her light escape
Into the beautiful.

THE BEE is not afraid of me,
I know the butterfly;
The pretty people in the woods
Receive me cordially.

The brooks laugh louder when I come,
The breezes madder play.
Wherefore, mine eyes, thy silver mists?
Wherefore, O summer's day?

PRESENTIMENT IS that long shadow on the lawn
Indicative that suns go down;
The notice to the startled grass
That darkness is about to pass.

I'LL TELL you how the sun rose,—
A ribbon at a time.
The steeples swam in amethyst,
The news like squirrels ran.

The hills untied their bonnets,
The bobolinks begun.
Then I said softly to myself,
"That must have been the sun!"

But how he set, I know not.
There seemed a purple stile
Which little yellow boys and girls
Were climbing all the while

Till when they reached the other side,
A dominie in gray
Put gently up the evening bars,
And led the flock away.

OF ALL the sounds despatched abroad,
There's not a charge to me
Like that old measure in the boughs,
That phraseless melody

The wind does, working like a hand
Whose fingers comb the sky,
Then quiver down, with tufts of tune
Permitted gods and me.

Inheritance it is to us
Beyond the art to earn,
Beyond the trait to take away
By robber, since the gain

Is gotten not of fingers,
And inner than the bone,
Hid golden for the whole of days,
And even in the urn

I cannot vouch the merry dust
Do not arise and play
In some odd pattern of its own
Some quainter holiday.

When winds go round and round in bands,
And thrum upon the door,
And birds take places overhead,
To bear them orchestra.

I crave him grace of summer boughs,
If such an outcast be,
Who never heard that fleshless chant
Rise solemn on the tree,

As if some caravan of sound
Off deserts, in the sky,
Had parted rank,
Then knit, and swept
In seamless company.

These are the days when birds come back,
A very few, a bird or two,
To take a backward look.

These are the days when skies put on
The old, old sophistries of June,—
A blue and gold mistake.

Oh, fraud that cannot cheat the bee,
Almost thy plausibility
Induces my belief,

Till ranks of seeds their witness bear,
And softly through the altered air
Hurries a timid leaf!

Oh, sacrament of summer days,
Oh, last communion in the haze,
Permit a child to join,

Thy sacred emblems to partake,
Thy consecrated bread to break,
Taste thine immortal wine!

———◦૪◦———

There's a certain slant of light,
On winter afternoons,
That oppresses, like the weight
Of cathedral tunes.

Heavenly hurt it gives us;
We can find no scar,
But internal difference
Where the meanings are.

None may teach it anything,
'Tis the seal, despair,—
An imperial affliction
Sent us of the air.

When it comes, the landscape listens,
Shadows hold their breath;
When it goes, 'tis like the distance
On the look of death.

A LIGHT EXISTS in spring
Not present on the year
At any other period.
When March is scarcely here

A color stands abroad
On solitary hills
That science cannot overtake,
But human nature feels.

It waits upon the lawn;
It shows the furthest tree
Upon the furthest slope we know;
It almost speaks to me.

Then, as horizons step,
Or noons report away,
Without the formula of sound,
It passes, and we stay:

A quality of loss
Affecting our content,
As trade had suddenly encroached
Upon a sacrament.

***

The spider as an artist
Has never been employed
Though his surpassing merit
Is freely certified

By every broom and Bridget
Throughout a Christian land.
Neglected son of genius,
I take thee by the hand.

***

To make a prairie it takes a clover and one bee,—
And revery.
The revery alone will do
If bees are few.

***

OF BRONZE and blaze
The north, to-night!
So adequate its forms,
So preconcerted with itself,
So distant to alarms,—
An unconcern so sovereign
To universe, or me,
It paints my simple spirit
With tints of majesty,
Till I take vaster attitudes,
And strut upon my stem,
Disdaining men and oxygen,
For arrogance of them.

The splendors are menagerie;
But their completeless show
Will entertain the centuries
When I am, long ago,
An island in dishonored grass,
Whom none but daisies know.

MINE BY the right of the white election!
Mine by the royal seal!
Mine by the sign in the scarlet prison
Bars cannot conceal!

Mine, here in vision and in veto!
Mine, by the grave's repeal
Titled, confirmed,—delirious charter!
Mine, while the ages steal!

If you were coming in the fall,
I'd brush the summer by
With half a smile and half a spurn,
As housewives do a fly.

If I could see you in a year,
I'd wind the months in balls,
And put them each in separate drawers,
Until their time befalls.

If only centuries delayed,
I'd count them on my hand,
Subtracting till my fingers dropped
Into Van Diemen's land.

If certain, when this life was out,
That yours and mine should be,
I'd toss it yonder like a rind,
And taste eternity.

But now, all ignorant of the length
Of time's uncertain wing,
It goads me, like the goblin bee,
That will not state its sting.

As if some little Arctic flower,
Upon the polar hem,
Went wandering down the latitudes,
Until it puzzled came
To continents of summer,
To firmaments of sun,
To strange, bright crowds of flowers,
And birds of foreign tongue!
I say, as if this little flower
To Eden wandered in—
What then? Why, nothing, only
Your inference therefrom!

I cannot live with you,
It would be life,
And life is over there
Behind the shelf

The sexton keeps the key to,
Putting up
Our life, his porcelain,
Like a cup

Discarded of the housewife,
Quaint or broken;
A newer Sèvres pleases,
Old ones crack.

I could not die with you,
For one must wait
To shut the other's gaze down,—
You could not.

And I, could I stand by
And see you freeze,
Without my right of frost,
Death's privilege?

Nor could I rise with you,
Because your face
Would put out Jesus',
That new grace

Glow plain and foreign
On my homesick eye,
Except that you, than he
Shone closer by.

They'd judge us—how?
For you served Heaven, you know,
Or sought to;
I could not,

Because you saturated sight,
And I had no more eyes
For sordid excellence
As Paradise.

And were you lost, I would be,
Though my name
Rang loudest
On the heavenly fame.

And were you saved,
And I condemned to be
Where you were not,
That self were hell to me.

So we must keep apart,
You there, I here,
With just the door ajar
That oceans are,
And prayer,
And that pale sustenance,
Despair!

———

THERE CAME a day at summer's full
Entirely for me;
I thought that such were for the saints,
Where revelations be.

The sun, as common, went abroad,
The flowers, accustomed, blew,
As if no sail the solstice passed
That maketh all things new.

The time was scarce profaned by speech;
The symbol of a word
Was needless, as at sacrament
The wardrobe of our Lord.

Each was to each the sealéd church,
Permitted to commune this time,
Lest we too awkward show
At supper of the Lamb.

The hours slid fast, as hours will,
Clutched tight by greedy hands;
So faces on two decks look back,
Bound to opposing lands.

And so, when all the time had failed,
Without external sound,
Each bound the other's crucifix,
We gave no other bond.

Sufficient troth that we shall rise—
Deposed, at length, the grave—
To that new marriage, justified
Through Calvaries of Love!

I'M CEDED, I've stopped being theirs;
The name they dropped upon my face
With water, in the country church
Is finished using now,
And they can put it with my dolls,
My childhood, and the string of spools
I've finished threading too.

Baptized before without the choice,
But this time consciously, of grace
Unto supremest name,
Called to my full, the crescent dropped,
Existence whole arc filled up
With one small diadem.

My second rank, too small the first,
Crowned, crowing on my father's breast,
A half unconscious queen;
But this time, adequate, erect,
With will to choose or to reject,
And I choose—just a throne.

―――⟋の⟍―――

COME SLOWLY, Eden!
Lips unused to thee,
Bashful, sip thy jasmines,
As the fainting bee,

Reaching late his flower,
Round her chamber hums,
Counts his nectars—enters,
And is lost in balms!

———⟋⟍———

I GAVE MYSELF to him,
And took himself for pay.
The solemn contract of a life
Was ratified this way.

The wealth might disappoint,
Myself a poorer prove
Than this great purchaser suspect,
The daily own of Love

Depreciate the vision;
But, till the merchant buy,
Still fable, in the isles of spice,
The subtle cargoes lie.

At least, 'tis mutual risk,—
Some found it mutual gain;
Sweet debt of Life,—each night to owe,
Insolvent, every noon.

———⟋⟍———

WILD NIGHTS! Wild nights!
Were I with thee,
Wild nights should be
Our luxury!

Futile the winds
To a heart in port,—
Done with the compass,
Done with the chart.

Rowing in Eden!
Ah! the sea!
Might I but moor
To-night in thee!

———— ✿ ————

SPLIT THE lark and you'll find the music,
Bulb after bulb, in silver rolled,
Scantily dealt to the summer morning,
Saved for your ear when lutes be old.

Loose the flood, you shall find it patent,
Gush after gush, reserved for you;
Scarlet experiment! sceptic Thomas,
Now, do you doubt that your bird was true?

———— ✿ ————

THE BRAIN within its groove
Runs evenly and true;
But let a splinter swerve,
'Twere easier for you
To put the water back
When floods have slit the hills,
And scooped a turnpike for themselves,
And blotted out the mills!

———⧖———

I MEANT TO have but modest needs,
Such as content, and heaven;
Within my income these could lie,
And life and I keep even.

But since the last included both,
It would suffice my prayer
But just for one to stipulate,
And grace would grant the pair.

And so, upon this wise I prayed,
Great Spirit, give to me
A heaven not so large as yours,
But large enough for me.

A smile suffused Jehovah's face;
The cherubim withdrew;
Grave saints stole out to look at me,
And showed their dimples, too.

I left the place with all my might,
My prayer away I threw;
The quiet ages picked it up,
And Judgment twinkled, too,

That one so honest be extant
As take the tale for true
That "Whatsoever you shall ask,
Itself be given you."

But I, grown shrewder, scan the skies
With a suspicious air,
As children, swindled for the first,
All swindlers be, infer.

REMORSE is memory awake,
Her companies astir,—
A presence of departed acts
At window and at door.

It's past set down before the soul,
And lighted with a match,
Perusal to facilitate
Of its condensed despatch.

Remorse is cureless,—the disease
Not even God can heal;
For 'tis His institution,
The complement of hell.

To learn the transport by the pain,
As blind men learn the sun;
To die of thirst, suspecting
That brooks in meadows run;

To stay the homesick, homesick feet
Upon a foreign shore
Haunted by native lands, the while,
And blue, beloved air—

This is the sovereign anguish,
This, the signal woe!
These are the patient laureates
Whose voices, trained below,

Ascend in ceaseless carol,
Inaudible, indeed,
To us, the duller scholars
Of the mysterious bard!

———⟨ᴥ⟩———

I years had been from home,
And now, before the door,
I dared not open, lest a face
I never saw before

Stare vacant into mine
And ask my business there.
My business,—just a life I left,
Was such still dwelling there?

I fumbled at my nerve,
I scanned the windows near;
The silence like an ocean rolled,
And broke against my ear.

I laughed a wooden laugh
That I could fear a door,
Who danger and the dead had faced,
But never quaked before.

I fitted to the latch
My hand, with trembling care,
Lest back the awful door should spring,
And leave me standing there.

I moved my fingers off
As cautiously as glass,
And held my ears, and like a thief
Fled gasping from the house.

SUPERIORITY TO fate
Is difficult to learn.
'Tis not conferred by any,
But possible to earn

A pittance at a time,
Until, to her surprise,
The soul with strict economy
Subsists till Paradise.

HEAVEN IS what I cannot reach!
The apple on the tree,
Provided it do hopeless hang,
That "heaven" is, to me.

The color on the cruising cloud,
The interdicted ground
Behind the hill, the house behind,—
There Paradise is found!

I HAD A guinea golden;
I lost it in the sand,
And though the sum was simple,
And pounds were in the land,
Still had it such a value
Unto my frugal eye,
That when I could not find it
I sat me down to sigh.

I had a crimson robin
Who sang full many a day,
But when the woods were painted
He, too, did fly away.
Time brought me other robins,—
Their ballads were the same,—
Still for my missing troubadour
I kept the "house at hame."

I had a star in heaven;
One Pleiad was its name,
And when I was not heeding
It wandered from the same.
And though the skies are crowded,
And all the night ashine,
I do not care about it,
Since none of them are mine.

My story has a moral:
I have a missing friend,—
Pleiad its name, and robin,
And guinea in the sand,—
And when this mournful ditty,
Accompanied with tear,
Shall meet the eye of traitor
In country far from here,
Grant that repentance solemn
May seize upon his mind,
And he no consolation
Beneath the sun may find.

———◦◦———

I MEASURE EVERY grief I meet
With analytic eyes;
I wonder if it weighs like mine,
Or has an easier size.

I wonder if they bore it long,
Or did it just begin?
I could not tell the date of mine,
It feels so old a pain.

I wonder if it hurts to live,
And if they have to try,
And whether, could they choose between,
They would not rather die.

I wonder if when years have piled—
Some thousands—on the cause
Of early hurt, if such a lapse
Could give them any pause;

Or would they go on aching still
Through centuries above,
Enlightened to a larger pain
By contrast with the love.

The grieved are many, I am told;
The reason deeper lies,—
Death is but one and comes but once,
And only nails the eyes.

There's grief of want, and grief of cold,
A sort they call "despair";
There's banishment from native eyes,
In sight of native air.

And though I may not guess the kind
Correctly, yet to me
A piercing comfort it affords
In passing Calvary,

To note the fashions of the cross,
Of those that stand alone,
Still fascinated to presume
That some are like my own.

———⟨⟩———

To LOSE one's faith surpasses
The loss of an estate,
Because estates can be
Replenished,—faith cannot.

Inherited with life,
Belief but once can be;
Annihilate a single clause,
And Being's beggary.

———⟨⟩———

I WORKED FOR chaff, and earning wheat
Was haughty and betrayed.
What right had fields to arbitrate
In matters ratified?

I tasted wheat,—and hated chaff,
And thanked the ample friend;
Wisdom is more becoming viewed
At distance than at hand.

———

Remembrance has a rear and front,—
'Tis something like a house;
It has a garret also
For refuge and the mouse,

Besides, the deepest cellar
That ever mason hewed;
Look to it, by its fathoms
Ourselves be not pursued.

———

Who never wanted,—maddest joy
Remains to him unknown;
The banquet of abstemiousness
Surpasses that of wine.

Within its hope, though yet ungrasped
Desire's perfect goal,
No nearer, lest reality
Should disenthrall thy soul.

———

SOFTENED BY Time's consummate plush,
How sleek the woe appears
That threatened childhood's citadel
And undermined the years!

Bisected now by bleaker griefs,
We envy the despair
That threatened childhood's citadel
So easy to repair.

THE SUN just touched the morning;
The morning, happy thing,
Supposed that he had come to dwell,
And life would be all spring.

She felt herself supremer,—
A raised, ethereal thing;
Henceforth for her what holiday!
Meanwhile, her wheeling king

Trailed slow along the orchards
His haughty, spangled hems,
Leaving a new necessity,—
The want of diadems!

The morning fluttered, staggered,
Felt feebly for her crown,—
Her unanointed forehead
Henceforth her only one.

From cocoon forth a butterfly
As lady from her door
Emerged—a summer afternoon—
Repairing everywhere,

Without design, that I could trace,
Except to stray abroad
On miscellaneous enterprise
The clovers understood.

Her pretty parasol was seen
Contracting in a field
Where men made hay, then struggling hard
With an opposing cloud,

Where parties, phantom as herself,
To Nowhere seemed to go
In purposeless circumference,
As 'twere a tropic show.

And notwithstanding bee that worked,
And flower that zealous blew,
This audience of idleness
Disdained them, from the sky,

Till sundown crept, a steady tide,
And men that made the hay,
And afternoon, and butterfly,
Extinguished in its sea.

To HEAR an oriole sing
May be a common thing,
Or only a divine.

It is not of the bird
Who sings the same, unheard,
As unto crowd.

The fashion of the ear
Attireth that it hear
In dun or fair.

So whether it be rune,
Or whether it be none,
Is of within;

The "tune is in the tree,"
The sceptic showeth me;
"No, sir! In thee!"

IT SIFTS from leaden sieves,
It powders all the wood,
It fills with alabaster wool
The wrinkles of the road.

It makes an even face
Of mountain and of plain,—
Unbroken forehead from the east
Unto the east again.

It reaches to the fence,
It wraps it, rail by rail,
Till it is lost in fleeces;
It flings a crystal veil

On stump and stack and stem,—
The summer's empty room,
Acres of seams where harvests were,
Recordless, but for them.

It ruffles wrists of posts,
As ankles of a queen,—
Then stills its artisans like ghosts,
Denying they have been.

Some keep the Sabbath going to church;
I keep it staying at home,
With a bobolink for a chorister,
And an orchard for a dome.

Some keep the Sabbath in surplice;
I just wear my wings,
And instead of tolling the bell for church,
Our little sexton sings.

God preaches,—a noted clergyman,—
And the sermon is never long;
So instead of getting to heaven at last,
I'm going all along!

WHAT MYSTERY pervades a well!
The water lives so far,
Like neighbor from another world
Residing in a jar.

The grass does not appear afraid;
I often wonder he
Can stand so close and look so bold
At what is dread to me.

Related somehow they may be,—
The sedge stands next the sea,
Where he is floorless, yet of fear
No evidence gives he.

But nature is a stranger yet;
The ones that cite her most
Have never passed her haunted house,
Nor simplified her ghost.

To pity those that know her not
Is helped by the regret
That those who know her, know her less
The nearer her they get.

I'VE SEEN a dying eye
Run round and round a room
In search of something, as it seemed,
Then cloudier become;

And then, obscure with fog,
And then be soldered down,
Without disclosing what it be,
'Twere blessed to have seen.

Let down the bars, O Death!
The tired flocks come in
Whose bleating ceases to repeat,
Whose wandering is done.

Thine is the stillest night,
Thine the securest fold;
Too near thou art for seeking thee,
Too tender to be told.

There is a shame of nobleness
Confronting sudden pelf,—
A finer shame of ecstasy
Convicted of itself.

A best disgrace a brave man feels,
Acknowledged of the brave,—
One more "Ye Blessed" to be told;
But this involves the grave.

If ANYBODY's friend be dead,
It's sharpest of the theme
The thinking how they walked alive,
At such and such a time.

Their costume, of a Sunday,
Some manner of the hair,—
A prank nobody knew but them,
Lost, in the sepulchre.

How warm they were on such a day:
You almost feel the date,
So short way off it seems; and now,
They're centuries from that.

How pleased they were at what you said;
You try to touch the smile,
And dip your fingers in the frost:
When was it, can you tell,

You asked the company to tea,
Acquaintance, just a few,
And chatted close with this grand thing
That don't remember you?

Past bows and invitations,
Past interview, and vow,
Past what ourselves can estimate,—
That makes the quick of woe!

THIS WORLD is not conclusion;
A sequel stands beyond,
Invisible, as music,
But positive, as sound.
It beckons and it baffles;
Philosophies don't know,
And through a riddle, at the last,
Sagacity must go.
To guess it puzzles scholars;
To gain it, men have shown
Contempt of generations,
And crucifixion known.

———◦◦———

IMMORTAL IS an ample word
When what we need is by,
But when it leaves us for a time,
'Tis a necessity.

Of heaven above the firmest proof
We fundamental know,
Except for its marauding hand,
It had been heaven below.

———◦◦———

Bereaved of all, I went abroad,
No less bereaved to be
Upon a new peninsula,—
The grave preceded me,

Obtained my lodgings ere myself,
And when I sought my bed,
The grave it was, reposed upon
The pillow for my head.

I waked, to find it first awake,
I rose,—it followed me;
I tried to drop it in the crowd,
To lose it in the sea,

In cups of artificial drowse
To sleep its shape away,—
The grave was finished, but the spade
Remained in memory.

He fumbles at your spirit
As players at the keys
Before they drop full music on;
He stuns you by degrees,

Prepares your brittle substance
For the ethereal blow,
By fainter hammers, further heard,
Then nearer, then so slow

Your breath has time to straighten,
Your brain to bubble cool,—
Deals one imperial thunderbolt
That scalps your naked soul.

———◦◦◦———

Safe in their alabaster chambers,
Untouched by morning and untouched by noon,
Sleep the meek members of the resurrection,
Rafter of satin, and roof of stone.

Light laughs the breeze in her castle of sunshine;
Babbles the bee in a stolid ear;
Pipe the sweet birds in ignorant cadence,—
Ah, what sagacity perished here!

Grand go the years in the crescent above them;
Worlds scoop their arcs, and firmaments row,
Diadems drop and Doges surrender,
Soundless as dots on a disk of snow.

———◦◦◦———

My cocoon tightens, colors tease,
I'm feeling for the air;
A dim capacity for wings
Degrades the dress I wear.

A power of butterfly must be
The aptitude to fly,
Meadows of majesty concedes
And easy sweeps of sky.

So I must baffle at the hint
And cipher at the sign,
And make much blunder, if at last
I take the clew divine.

———————

EXULTATION IS the going
Of an inland soul to sea,—
Past the houses, past the headlands,
Into deep eternity!

Bred as we, among the mountains,
Can the sailor understand
The divine intoxication
Of the first league out from land?

———————

I DIED FOR beauty, but was scarce
Adjusted in the tomb,
When one who died for truth was lain
In an adjoining room.

He questioned softly why I failed?
"For beauty," I replied.
"And I for truth,—the two are one;
We brethren are," he said.

And so, as kinsmen met a night,
We talked between the rooms,
Until the moss had reached our lips,
And covered up our names.

I LIKE A look of agony,
Because I know it's true;
Men do not sham convulsion,
Nor simulate a throe.

The eyes glaze once, and that is death.
Impossible to feign
The beads upon the forehead
By homely anguish strung.

———⟆⟅———

I REASON, EARTH is short,
And anguish absolute,
And many hurt;
But what of that?

I reason, we could die:
The best vitality
Cannot excel decay;
But what of that?

I reason that in heaven
Somehow, it will be even,
Some new equation given;
But what of that?

———⟆⟅———

THE SUN kept setting, setting still;
No hue of afternoon
Upon the village I perceived,—
From house to house 'twas noon.

The dusk kept dropping, dropping still;
No dew upon the grass,
But only on my forehead stopped,
And wandered in my face.

My feet kept drowsing, drowsing still,
My fingers were awake;
Yet why so little sound myself
Unto my seeming make?

How well I knew the light before!
I could not see it now.
'Tis dying, I am doing; but
I'm not afraid to know.

DEATH IS a dialogue between
The spirit and the dust.
"Dissolve," says Death. The Spirit, "Sir,
I have another trust."

Death doubts it, argues from the ground.
The Spirit turns away,
Just laying off, for evidence,
An overcoat of clay.

I NEVER LOST as much but twice,
And that was in the sod;
Twice have I stood a beggar
Before the door of God!

Angels, twice descending,
Reimbursed my store.
Burglar, banker, father,
I am poor once more!

AT LEAST to pray is left, is left.
O Jesus! in the air
I know not which thy chamber is,—
I'm knocking everywhere.

Thou stirrest earthquake in the South,
And maelstrom in the sea;
Say, Jesus Christ of Nazareth,
Hast thou no arm for me?

DEATH SETS a thing significant
The eye had hurried by,
Except a perished creature
Entreat us tenderly

To ponder little workmanships
In crayon or in wool,
With "This was last her fingers did,"
Industrious until

The thimble weighed too heavy,
The stitches stopped themselves,
And then 'twas put among the dust
Upon the closet shelves.

A book I have, a friend gave,
Whose pencil, here and there,
Had notched the place that pleased him,—
At rest his fingers are.

Now, when I read, I read not,
For interrupting tears
Obliterate the etchings
Too costly for repairs.

THEIR HEIGHT in heaven comforts not,
Their glory nought to me;
'Twas best imperfect, as it was;
I'm finite, I can't see.

The house of supposition,
The glimmering frontier
That skirts the acres of perhaps,
To me shows insecure.

The wealth I had contented me;
If 'twas a meaner size,
Then I had counted it until
It pleased my narrow eyes

Better than larger values,
However true their show;
This timid life of evidence
Keeps pleading, "I don't know."

———— ∽∽ ————

Our journey had advanced;
Our feet were almost come
To that odd fork in Being's road,
Eternity by term.

Our pace took sudden awe,
Our feet reluctant led.
Before were cities, but between,
The forest of the dead.

Retreat was out of hope,—
Behind, a sealéd route,
Eternity's white flag before,
And God at every gate.

———— ∽∽ ————

ESSENTIAL OILS are wrung:
The attar from the rose
Is not expressed by suns alone,
It is the gift of screws.

The general rose decays;
But this, in lady's drawer,
Makes summer when the lady lies
In ceaseless rosemary.

ONE NEED not be a chamber to be haunted,
One need not be a house;
The brain has corridors surpassing
Material place.

Far safer, of a midnight meeting
External ghost,
Than an interior confronting
That whiter host.

Far safer through an Abbey gallop,
The stones achase,
Than, moonless, one's own self encounter
In lonesome place.

Ourself, behind ourself concealed,
Should startle most;
Assassin, hid in our apartment,
Be horror's least.

The prudent carries a revolver,
He bolts the door,
O'erlooking a superior spectre
More near.

———❦———

It was not death, for I stood up,
And all the dead lie down;
It was not night, for all the bells
Put out their tongues, for noon.

It was not frost, for on my flesh
I felt siroccos crawl,—
Nor fire, for just my marble feet
Could keep a chancel cool

And yet it tasted like them all;
The figures I have seen
Set orderly, for burial,
Reminded me of mine,

As if my life were shaven
And fitted to a frame,
And could not breathe without a key;
And 'twas like midnight, some,

When everything that ticked has stopped,
And space stares, all around,
Or grisly frosts, first autumn morns,
Repeal the beating ground.

But most like chaos,—stopless, cool,—
Without a chance or spar,
Or even a report of land
To justify despair.

———————

GREAT STREETS of silence led away
To neighborhoods of pause;
Here was no notice, no dissent,
No universe, no laws.

By clocks 'twas morning, and for night
The bells at distance called;
But epoch had no basis here,
For period exhaled.

———————

AFTER A hundred years
Nobody knows the place,—
Agony, that enacted there,
Motionless as peace.

Weeds triumphant ranged,
Strangers strolled and spelled
At the lone orthography
Of the elder dead.

Winds of summer fields
Recollect the way,—
Instinct picking up the key
Dropped by memory.

THE GRAVE my little cottage is,
Where, keeping house for thee,
I make my parlor orderly,
And lay the marble tea,

For two divided, briefly,
A cycle, it may be,
Till everlasting life unite
In strong society.

———⌾———

THEY SAY that "time assuages,"—
Time never did assuage;
An actual suffering strengthens,
As sinews do, with age.

Time is a test of trouble,
But not a remedy.
If such it prove, it prove too
There was no malady.

———⌾———

THE STIMULUS, beyond the grave
His countenance to see,
Supports me like imperial drams
    Afforded royalty.

THE DISTANCE that the dead have gone
Does not at first appear;
Their coming back seems possible
For many an ardent year.

And then, that we have followed them
We more than half suspect,
So intimate have we become
With their dear retrospect.

EACH THAT we lose takes part of us;
A crescent still abides,
Which like the moon, some turbid night,
Is summoned by the tides.

ME! COME! My dazzled face
In such a shining place!

Me! Hear! My foreign ear
The sounds of welcome near!

The saints shall meet
Our bashful feet.

My holiday shall be
That they remember me;

My paradise, the fame
That they pronounce my name.

I FELT A funeral in my brain,
And mourners, to and fro,
Kept treading, treading, till it seemed
That sense was breaking through

And when they all were seated,
A service like a drum
Kept beating, beating, till I thought
My mind was going numb.

And then I heard them lift a box,
And creak across my soul
With those same boots of lead, again.
Then space began to toll

As all the heavens were a bell,
And Being but an ear,
And I and silence some strange race,
Wrecked, solitary, here.

I HEARD A fly buzz when I died;
The stillness round my form
Was like the stillness in the air
Between the heaves of storm.

The eyes beside had wrung them dry,
And breaths were gathering sure
For that last onset, when the king
Be witnessed in his power.

I willed my keepsakes, signed away
What portion of me I
Could make assignable,—and then
There interposed a fly,

With blue, uncertain, stumbling buzz,
Between the light and me;
And then the windows failed, and then
I could not see to see.

———✦———

THERE'S BEEN a death in the opposite house
As lately as to-day.
I know it by the numb look
Such houses have alway.

The neighbors rustle in and out,
The doctor drives away.
A window opens like a pod,
Abrupt, mechanically;

Somebody flings a mattress out,—
The children hurry by;
They wonder if It died on that,—
I used to when a boy.

The minister goes stiffly in
As if the house were his,
And he owned all the mourners now,
And little boys besides;

And then the milliner, and the man
Of the appalling trade,
To take the measure of the house.
There'll be that dark parade

Of tassels and of coaches soon;
It's easy as a sign,—
The intuition of the news
In just a country town.

———⟨∽⟩———

A CLOCK STOPPED—not the mantel's;
Geneva's farthest skill
Can't put the puppet bowing
That just now dangled still.

An awe came on the trinket!
The figures hunched with pain,
Then quivered out of decimals
Into degreeless noon.

It will not stir for doctors,
This pendulum of snow;
The shopman importunes it,
While cool, concernless No

Nods from the gilded pointers,
Nods from the seconds slim,
Decades of arrogance between
The dial life and him.

FAR FROM love the Heavenly Father
Leads the chosen child;
Oftener through realm of briar
Than the meadow mild,

Oftener by the claw of dragon
Than the hand of friend,
Guides the little one predestined
To the native land.

———— ⚶ ————

ON THIS wondrous sea,
Sailing silently,
Knowest thou the shore
Ho! pilot, ho!
Where no breakers roar,
Where the storm is o'er?

In the silent west
Many sails at rest,
Their anchors fast;
Thither I pilot thee,—
Land, ho! Eternity!
Ashore at last!

———— ⚶ ————

THE SOUL that has a Guest,
Does seldom go abroad,
Diviner Crowd at home
Obliterate the need,
And courtesy forbid
A Host's departure, when
Upon Himself be visiting
The Emperor of Men!

FAME IS a fickle food
Upon a shifting plate,
Whose table once a Guest, but not
The second time, is set.

Whose crumbs the crows inspect,
And with ironic caw
Flap past it to the Farmer's corn;
Men eat of it and die.

PERCEPTION OF an
Object costs
Precise the Object's loss.
Perception in itself a gain
Replying to its price;
The Object Absolute is nought,
Perception sets it fair,
And then upbraids a Perfectness
That situates so far.

THERE IS another Loneliness
That many die without,
Not want or friend occasions it,
Or circumstance or lot.

But nature sometimes, sometimes thought,
And whoso it befall
Is richer than could be divulged
By mortal numeral.

THE MISSING All prevented me
From missing minor things.
If nothing larger than a World's
Departure from a hinge,
Or Sun's extinction be observed,
'Twas not so large that I
Could lift my forehead from my work
For curiosity.

THE PROPS assist the house
Until the house is built,
And then the props withdraw—
And adequate, erect,
The house supports itself;
Ceasing to recollect
The auger and the carpenter.
Just such a retrospect
Hath the perfected life,
A past of plank and nail,
And slowness,—then the scaffolds drop—
Affirming it a soul.

THE SOUL's superior instants
Occur to Her alone,
When friend and earth's occasion
Have infinite withdrawn.

Or she, Herself, ascended
To too remote a height,
For lower recognition
Than Her Omnipotent.

This mortal abolition
Is seldom, but as fair
As Apparition—subject
To autocratic air.

Eternity's disclosure
To favorites, a few,
Of the Colossal substance
Of immortality.

BEAUTY CROWDS me till I die,
Beauty, mercy have on me!
But if I expire today,
Let it be in sight of thee.

The Moon upon her fluent route
Defiant of a road,
The stars Etruscan argument,
Substantiate a God.
If Aims impel these Astral Ones,
The Ones allowed to know,
Know that which makes them as forgot
As Dawn forgets them now.

In winter, in my room,
I came upon a worm,
Pink, lank, and warm.
But as he was a worm
And worms presume,
Not quite with him at home—
Secured him by a string
To something neighboring,
And went along.

A trifle afterward
A thing occurred,
I'd not believe it if I heard—
But state with creeping blood;
A snake, with mottles rare,
Surveyed my chamber floor,
In feature as the worm before,
But ringed with power.

The very string
With which I tied him, too,
When he was mean and new,
That string was there.

I shrank—"How fair you are!"
Propitiation's claw—
"Afraid?" he hissed,
"Of me?"
"No cordiality?"
He fathomed me.
Then, to a rhythm slim
Secreted in his form,
As patterns swim,
Projected him.

That time I flew,
Both eyes his way,
Lest he pursue—
Nor ever ceased to run,
Till, in a distant town,
Towns on from mine—
I sat me down;
This was a dream.

THIS QUIET Dust was Gentlemen and Ladies,
And Lads and Girls;
Was laughter and ability and sighing,
And frocks and curls.
This passive place a Summer's nimble mansion,
Where Bloom and Bees
Fulfilled their Oriental Circuit,
Then ceased like these.

THE DEVIL, had he fidelity,
Would be the finest friend—
Because he has ability,
But Devils cannot mend.
Perfidy is the virtue
That would he but resign,—
The Devil, so amended,
Were durably divine.

"HEAVENLY FATHER," take to Thee
The supreme iniquity,
Fashioned by Thy candid hand
In a moment contraband.
Though to trust us seem to us
More respectful—"we are dust."
We apologize to Thee
For Thine own Duplicity.

THE BIBLE is an antique volume
Written by faded men,
At the suggestion of Holy Spectres—
Subjects—Bethlehem—
Eden—the ancient Homestead—
Satan—the Brigadier,
Judas—the great Defaulter,
David—the Troubadour.
Sin—a distinguished Precipice
Others must resist,
Boys that "believe"
Are very lonesome—
Other boys are "lost."
Had but the tale a warbling Teller
All the boys would come—
Orpheus' sermon captivated,
It did not condemn.

———◦◦◦———

THAT LOVE is all there is,
Is all we know of Love;
It is enough, the freight should be
Proportioned to the groove.

———◦◦◦———

Publication is the auction
Of the mind of man,
Poverty be justifying
For so foul a thing.

Possibly,—but we would rather
From our garret go
White unto the White Creator,
Than invest our snow.

Thought belongs to Him who gave it—
Then to him who bear
Its corporeal illustration.
Sell the Royal air
In the parcel,—be the merchant
Of the Heavenly Grace,
But reduce no human spirit
To disgrace of price!

I cannot dance upon my toes,
No man instructed me,
But often times among my mind
A glee possesseth me
That had I ballet knowledge
Would put itself abroad
In pirouette to blanch a troupe,
Or lay a Prima mad!

And though I had no gown of gauze,
No ringlet to my hair,
Nor hopped for audiences like birds,
One claw upon the air,—
Nor tossed my shape in eider balls,
Nor rolled on wheels of snow
Till I was out of sight in sound,
The house encored me so—
Nor any knew I know the art
I mention easy here—
Nor any placard boast me,
It's full as opera!

———————

COLOR, CASTE, Denomination—
These are Time's affair,
Death's division classifying
Does not know they are.

As in sleep—all here forgotten,
Tenets put behind,
Death's large democratic fingers
Rub away the brand.

If Circassian—He is careless—
If He put away
Chrysalis of Blonde or Umber,
Equal butterfly

They emerge from His obscuring;
What Death knows so well,
Our minuter intuitions
Deem incredible.

———— ❦ ————

I reckon, when I count at all,
First Poets—then the Sun—
Then Summer—then the Heaven of God—
And then the list is done.
But looking back—the first so seems
To comprehend the whole—
The others look a needless show,
So I write Poets—All.
This summer lasts a solid year,
They can afford a sun
The East would deem extravagant,
And if the final Heaven
Be beautiful as they disclose
To those who trust in them,
It is too difficult a grace
To justify the dream.

———— ❦ ————

THIS WAS a Poet—it is that
Distills amazing sense
From ordinary meanings,
And attars so immense

From the familiar species
That perished by the door,
We wonder it was not ourselves
Arrested it before.

Of pictures the discloser
The Poet, it is he,
Entitles us by contrast
To ceaseless poverty.

Of portion so unconscious
The robbing could not harm,
Himself, to him, a fortune
Exterior to Time.

———⟳———

EXPERIENCE IS the angled road
Preferred against the mind
By paradox, the mind itself
Presuming it to lead
Quite opposite. How complicate
The discipline of man,
Compelling him to choose himself
His pre-appointed pain.

———⟳———

A PRISON GETS to be a friend;
Between its ponderous face
And ours a kinsmanship exists,
And in its narrow eyes
We come to look with gratitude
For the appointed beam
It deals us—stated as our food,
And hungered for the same.

We learn to know the planks
That answer to our feet,
So miserable a sound at first
Nor even now so sweet
As plashing in the pools
When memory was a boy,
But a demurer circuit,
A geometric joy.

The posture of the key
That interrupts the day
To our endeavor,—not so real
The cheek of Liberty
As this companion steel,
Whose features day and night
Are present to us as our own
And as escapeless quite.

The narrow round, the stint,
The slow exchange of hope
For something passiver,—content
Too steep for looking up,
The liberty we knew
Avoided like a dream,
Too wide for any night but Heaven,
If that indeed redeem.

FOREVER is composed of Nows—
'Tis not a different time,
Except for infiniteness
And latitude of home.

From this, experienced here,
Remove the dates to these,
Let months dissolve in further months,
And years exhale in years.

Without certificate or pause
Or celebrated days,
As infinite our years would be
As Anno Domini's.

I DWELL IN Possibility,
A fairer house than Prose,
More numerous of windows,
Superior of doors.

Of chambers, as the cedars—
Impregnable of eye;
And for an everlasting roof
The gables of the sky.

Of visitors—the fairest—
For occupation—this—
The spreading wide my narrow hands
To gather Paradise.

———◦◦◦———

IT'S EASY to invent a life,
God does it every day—
Creation but a gambol
Of His authority.

It's easy to efface it,
The thrifty Deity
Could scarce afford eternity
To spontaneity.

The Perished Patterns murmur,
But His perturbless plan
Proceed—inserting here a Sun—
There—leaving out a Man.

I NEVER FELT at home below,
And in the handsome skies
I shall not feel at home I know,
I don't like Paradise.

Because it's Sunday all the time
And recess never comes,
And Eden'll be so lonesome
Bright Wednesday afternoons.

If God could make a visit,
Or ever took a nap—
So not to see us—but they say
Himself a telescope

Perennial beholds us,—
Myself would run away
From Him and Holy Ghost and All—
But—there's the Judgment Day!

———⟋⟍———

THE TINT I cannot take is best,
The color too remote
That I could show it in bazaar
A guinea at a sight—

The fine impalpable array
That swaggers on the eye
Like Cleopatra's company
Repeated in the sky—

The moments of dominion
That happen on the Soul
And leave it with a discontent
Too exquisite to tell—

The eager look on landscapes
As if they just repressed
Some secret that was pushing,
Like chariots, in the breast—

The pleading of the Summer,
That other prank of snow
That covers mystery with tulle
For fear the squirrels know—

Their graspless manners mock us,
Until the cheated eye
Shuts arrogantly in the grave,
Another way to see.

———◦ço———

THE DOOMED regard the sunrise
With different delight
Because when next it burns abroad
They doubt to witness it.

The man to die to-morrow
Detects the meadow bird,
Because its music stirs the axe
That clamors for his head.

Joyful to whom the sunrise
Precedes enamored day—
Joyful for whom the meadow bird
Has aught but elegy!

———◦∿◦———

OF NEARNESS to her sundered things
The Soul has special times,
When Dimness looks the oddity,
Distinctness easy seems.

The shapes we buried dwell about
Familiar in the rooms,
Untarnished by the sepulchre
Our moldering playmate comes

In just the jacket that he wore,
Long buttoned in the mold,
Since we, old mornings, children played,
Divided by a world.

The grave yields back her robberies,
The years are pilfered things,
Bright knots of apparitions
Salute us with their wings—

As we it were that perished,
Themselves had just remained
Till we rejoin them, and 'twas They
And not Ourselves that mourned.

Heaven is so far of the mind
That were the mind dissolved,
The site of it by architect
Could not again be proved.

'Tis vast as our capacity
As fair as our idea,
To him of adequate desire
No further 'tis than Here.

———◦◦———

The only news I know
Is bulletins all day
From Immortality.

The only shows I see
To-morrow and To-day,
Perchance Eternity.

The only One I meet
Is God,—the only street
Existence, this traversed

If other news there be,
Or admirabler show—
I'll tell it you.

———◦◦———

THE SOUL'S distinct connection
With immortality
Is best disclosed by danger,
Or quick calamity,—

As lightning on a landscape
Exhibits sheets of place
Not yet suspected but for flash
And bolt of suddenness.

PAIN EXPANDS the time,
Ages coil within
The minute circumference
Of a single brain.

Pain contracts the time
Occupied with shot,
Triplets of eternities
Are as they were not.

THE ADMIRATIONS
And contempts of time
Show justest through an open tomb—
The dying, as it were a height,
Reorganizes estimate,
And what we saw not
We distinguish clear,
And mostly see not

What we saw before.
'Tis compound vision—
Light enabling light—
The Finite furnished
With the Infinite—
Convex and concave witness,
Back toward time,
And forward toward
The God of Him.

My portion is defeat to-day
A paler luck than victory,
Less paeans, fewer bells—
The drums don't follow me with tunes,
Defeat a something dumber means,
More difficult than bells.
'Tis populous with bone and stain,
And men too straight to bend again,
And piles of solid moan,
And chips of blank in boyish eyes,
And shreds of prayer and death's surprise
Stamped visible in stone.
There's something prouder over there—
The trumpets tell it in the air.
How different victory to him
Who has it, and the One
Who to have had it would have been
Contenteder to die.

ON A columnar self
How ample to rely;
In tumult or extremity
How good the certainty

That lever cannot pry,
And wedge cannot divide
Conviction that the granite base,
Though none be on our side.

Suffice us, for a crowd,
Ourselves—and rectitude—
And that companion not far off
From furthest good man—
God.

I TOOK ONE draught of life,
I'll tell you what I paid,
Precisely an existence—
The market price, they said.

They weighed me, dust by dust,
They balanced film with film,
Then handed me my being's worth—
A single dram of Heaven.

ONE LIFE of so much consequence
That I for it would pay
My Soul's entire income
In ceaseless salary.
One pearl of such proportion
That I would instant dive
Although I knew to take it
Would cost me just a life.
The sea is full—I know it!
That does not blur my gem!
It burns distinct from all the row
Intact in diadem!
Oh, Life is thick—I know it!
Yet not so dense a crowd
But monarchs are perceptible
Far down the dustiest road!

———◦———

MY LIFE had stood a loaded gun
In corners, till a day
The owner passed—identified,
And carried me away.

And now we roam the sov'reign woods,
And now we hunt the doe—
And every time I speak for him
The mountains straight reply.

And do I smile, such cordial light
Upon the valley glow—
It is as a Vesuvian face
Had let its pleasure through.

And when at night, our good day done,
I guard my master's head,
'Tis better than the eider duck's
Deep pillow to have shared.

To foe of his I'm deadly foe,
None stir the second time
On whom I lay a yellow eye
Or an emphatic thumb.

Though I than he may longer live,
He longer must than I,
For I have but the art to kill—
Without the power to die.

———

WHY DO I love thee, Sir?
Because—
The wind does not
Require the grass
To answer wherefore, when
He pass,
She cannot keep her place.

The lightning never asked
An eye
Wherefore she shut
When he was by—
Because he knows
She cannot speak,
And reasons not contained
Of talk
There be—preferred by daintier folk.

Renunciation
Is a piercing virtue,
The letting go
A presence for an expectation—
Not now.

The putting out of eyes
Just sunrise,
Lest Day Day's great progenitor
Out-show.

Renunciation is the choosing
Against itself,
Itself to justify
Unto itself;
When larger function
Make that appear
Smaller, that sated vision
Here.

AFTER GREAT pain a formal feeling comes—
The nerves sit ceremonious like tombs;
The stiff Heart questions—was it He that bore?
And yesterday—or centuries before?

The feet mechanical
Go round a wooden way
Of ground or air or Ought, regardless grown,
A quartz contentment like a stone.

This is the hour of lead
Remembered if outlived,
As freezing persons recollect the snow—
First chill, then stupor, then the letting go.

———·———

THERE IS a pain so utter
It swallows Being up,
Then covers the abyss with trance
So memory can step
Around, across, upon it,
As One within a swoon
Goes steady, when an open eye
Would drop him bone by bone.

———·———

Because I could not stop for Death,
He kindly stopped for me;
The carriage held but just ourselves
And Immortality.

We slowly drove, he knew no haste,
And I had put away
My labor, and my leisure too,
For his civility.

We passed the school where children played
At wrestling in a ring;
We passed the fields of gazing grain,
We passed the setting sun.

We paused before a house that seemed
A swelling of the ground;
The roof was scarcely visible,
The cornice but a mound.

Since then 'tis centuries; but each
Feels shorter than the day
I first surmised the horses' heads
Were toward eternity.

BEHIND ME dips Eternity,
Before me Immortality,
Myself the term between—
Death but the drift of Eastern gray
Dissolving into dawn away
Before the West begins.

'Tis Kingdom—afterwards—they say,
In perfect pauseless monarchy,
Whose Prince is son of none—
Himself His dateless dynasty,
Himself Himself diversify
In duplicate divine.

'Tis Miracle before me then,
Then Miracle behind, between,—
A crescent is the sea
With midnight to the north of her
And midnight to the south of her,
And maelstrom in the sky.

INDEX OF FIRST LINES